People and nature in cities

A summary of the report
The social aspects of planning and managing natural parks in urban areas
for the Trust for Urban Ecology

Alison Millward and Barbara Mostyn

ISBN 0 86139 488 7

Designed by Meridian Creative Printed by Fisherprint 2M

The Nature Conservancy Council is the body responsible for advising Government on nature conservation in Great Britain. Its work includes the selection, establishment and management of National Nature Reserves; the selection and management of Marine Nature Reserves; the identification and notification of Sites of Special Scientific Interest; the provision of advice and dissemination of knowledge about nature conservation; and the support and conduct of research relevant to these functions.

This is one of a range of publications produced by Publicity Services Branch. A catalogue listing current titles is available from Dept UWA, Nature Conservancy Council, Northminster House, Peterborough PE1 1UA.

Contents

Introduction

As a result of recent initiatives to bring nature into the cities, many urban dwellers now have access to a range of natural open spaces that complement the traditional-style parks and recreational grounds typical of so much urban open space in this country. There are ecological parks, natural parks, nature reserves, green spaces, walkways and community nature parks where once there was just a forgotten field, wood, pond, quarry or scene of dereliction.

This change has occurred largely through the efforts of landscape architects and nature conservationists, with much encouragement from groups of local residents keen to protect and enhance natural open spaces in their neighbourhoods. As far as social considerations are concerned, these people have based their actions, in part, on the belief that because they enjoy natural landscapes, whether in the countryside or in the town, so too will others. But is this the case? What do people really think about these places, how do they use them, and do the answers to these questions match those anticipated by the landscape architects and conservationists?

This study was initiated by the Nature Conservancy Council (NCC) in order to answer some of the questions and pass on the results to those who plan, design and manage open spaces in urban areas. The basic question the research set out to answer was "How can the needs of people be accommodated on an urban wildlife site?" A great deal is known about the needs of nature, but the needs of people, for whom the sites are being designed, are under-researched and poorly understood. This study was designed to provide a better understanding of human behaviour and the attitudes motivating that behaviour in the context of an urban wildlife site.

The research focused on case studies of three sites –

Gillespie Road Park

This is a small, inner city site of nearly two hectares, in Islington, created from old railway sidings, and tucked away behind some Victorian terraced streets. Some of the existing brambles, lupins, rough grassland and birch scrub were retained, and a small pond, wildflower meadows and new woodland planting have been added. Good use is made of the picnic tables, benches and a kickabout area that have been provided and the site is managed by two wardens employed by the London Borough of Islington. Despite its small size, the site is used for a wide variety of activities. This is also a very friendly site where visitors seem to find it easy to strike up conversations with others and meet for joint activities such as the Nature Club and informal games of football.

Newbridge Farm Recreation Ground

This is a long linear, open space of four hectares that runs beside the River Cole in Birmingham and between private and council housing estates built in the 1930s. Following a period of disturbance from tipping and river works, the site has been left to develop naturally over the past 15 years. Rough grassland is prevalent here with patches of tall herbaceous perennials, such as tansy and cow parsley, hawthorn scrub and some close mown grass beside the roads. A few main drain pipes from the earlier river works remain. The site is owned by Birmingham City Council. At the time the research was undertaken the paths were unsurfaced, there were no amenities and the site was unwardened. Many people pass through this site on their way to the shops, bus stops and schools and seem to appreciate its natural features despite some obvious signs of neglect and abuse. Children and teenagers make good use of the site and find a degree of privacy that is just not possible on a smaller site such as Gillespie Road.

Birchwood Brook Park

This is a long linear, park of twelve hectares, that runs between the edge of the Oakwood housing estate and the Liverpool to Manchester railway line in Warrington New Town. In the past the site had been used as railway sidings and as a drainage area for the nearby ordnance factory (since demolished). The designers adopted a particularly comprehensive ecological approach, by thinning the existing ridge of birch woodland and introducing wildflower meadows and heathland. An extensive path system has been provided together with benches and a number of innovative amenities such as turf circles and circular wooden sitting areas. The site is managed by the New Town Corporation and the District Council provides rangers. It is used for a wide variety of purposes including walking, dog walking, jogging and cycling, and is a short cut to the station and shopping centre. Children are often to be found near the brook and playing in the undergrowth along the edge of the park near the housing.

Maps of the sites are reproduced in the Appendix.

This research tested some popular theories held by both ecologists and psychologists; why people think certain things about natural open spaces; why they do certain things in natural open spaces and fail to do others; and why they often do not do what they say they do. The findings of the research have been set out to clarify whether the results support or oppose these previously held theories. Further detail on the research can be found in the Appendix and in the full report published by the NCC.

Walking, talking and making contact with nature

A natural, seemingly unmanaged and unrestricted atmosphere was a prime goal for the first generation of public park designers of the 19th century, as well as for the designers of our three case study sites. However, throughout the 20th century many Victorian parks have become more formal and stylised. As the landscape planner of Gillespie Road Park put it –

> "I wanted to give the public a different open space to what they were used to, with the widest range of habitats. I was hoping that the kids and their parents would use the pond to see what was in it; and the bit of woodland just to feel they could run around in it and wouldn't be as restricted as in a traditional park."

It was found that all three sites were used for a wide range of mainly less energetic activities. Over 40% of users were either taking a stroll or walking the dog. Sitting and chatting with friends or watching the dog play proved popular at Gillespie Road and 29% of visitors to Newbridge Farm used the site as a through route. Of those engaged in more energetic pursuits such as cycling, jogging and ball games the greater proportion were males.

It would also seem that people do feel free to use the sites as they wish –

> "It's not all clipped and neat and laid out with cement; you feel free."

> "Natural, you can escape, nothing military about it."

However new-town dwellers, who often originate from inner city areas, were seen not to feel as comfortable and free in natural open space –

> "I have the feeling that people who come here from Liverpool or Manchester, they've never been to a place like this before. They're bowled over by so much green; they don't know what to do."

Unlike the situation in traditional style parks, females are not the heaviest users of natural open spaces. Birchwood Brook Park attracted the greatest percentage of 44%, followed by Gillespie Road with 43% and Newbridge Farm, the site with no wardens, with only 22%. It is also widely thought that parks are particularly attractive to parents with toddlers. This did not prove to be the case for our three sites, where only 3% of all visitors were parents accompanying toddlers. Socialising with friends or family members during a visit was more common than had been expected as two thirds of the visitors were observed to be accompanied by someone else, especially adults with children.

On the whole the general levels of use were low and perceived to be such by providers and users alike –

	Users per hour	
	Sundays	Weekdays
Birchwood Brook	5	4
Gillespie Road	7	6
Newbridge Farm	0	7

As regards the friendliness of a site, being willing to make contact with another visitor or indeed to visit alone requires secure, confident feelings to the extent that the site is regarded as 'my territory' not 'theirs' (the authorities) and this may account for why socialising was much less evident at Birchwood Brook Park, the new-town site. Another element of this issue has to do with perceptions of who else uses urban wildlife sites. Respondents to the questionnaire surveys, tended to describe users as stereotypes in terms of age group or activity. The elderly, mums with toddlers, teenagers, dog walkers and joggers were typically mentioned; but from the observation studies and except for dog walkers, they were not found to constitute major user groups. Adults and walkers constituted the main users but did not themselves recognise this fact.

Each site had a definite image in the mind of the local community. The major users of Newbridge Farm were considered to be teenagers, children and the elderly. Problem users were identified as teenage gangs, tippers, glue sniffers, flashers, gypsies and motorbikers. Gillespie Road was perceived to be used mainly by dog walkers, parents with children and toddlers, teenagers, the elderly and school groups. Problem users here were regarded as dogs, children on bikes, vandals, drunks and dirty old men. Dog walkers, the elderly, parents with children, joggers, walkers and cyclists were regarded as the main users of Birchwood Brook Park, and yet children on their own or in groups were found to make up 34% of all users of this site. Fewer problem users were identified for this new-town site than for the other two; only vandals, glue sniffers, a flasher and moped riders.

Of the visitors who were tracked over a maximum period of 30 minutes, 50% were seen to take an interest in the natural features of the sites, especially adults accompanying children, people visiting alone and even some of those who were obviously passing through. Birds, butterflies, moths, other insects, snails, ducks, flowers and pondlife seem to be of particular interest. Popular activities included stopping to look into the pond, hunting for insects in the meadows, picking berries and listening to bird song, particularly amongst men, despite the belief that environmental pastimes are thought to appeal more to women. The questionnaire surveys and group discussions confirmed that observing nature is an important motive for visiting an urban wildlife site and visitors are only too well aware of their ignorance about the flora and fauna and express a strong desire to find out more from leaflets and to have access to wardens "to explain things".

Despite the desire to create natural landscapes many designers, planners and parks managers, including those from our sites, express the concern that the public may find such sites untidy, infested and dangerous. Both frequent and occasional users thought this not to be the case; especially so amongst those from the Birmingham site which was unmanaged and suffered from tipping. Many felt that the diversity of trees, grass and shrubs, as opposed to short mown grass meant that "There's always something different every time you go there" and as a woman from Warrington said –

> "Where I actually walk the dog, I come off the main path and through the mown areas, through the trees and there are lots of little wild flowers, wild roses and hawthorn in blossom. The mown areas, through the long grass, take the flatness off it and I like the swirls in it. I like the brook being overgrown because I was watching a heron feeding from there, and lots of fishes and frogs. I prefer it to be slightly overgrown."

As discovered in previous research, users of natural open spaces in urban areas find them appealing for the same reasons that countryside recreation sites appeal – the naturalness, openness and freedom. Reasons given for why users liked the case sites were –

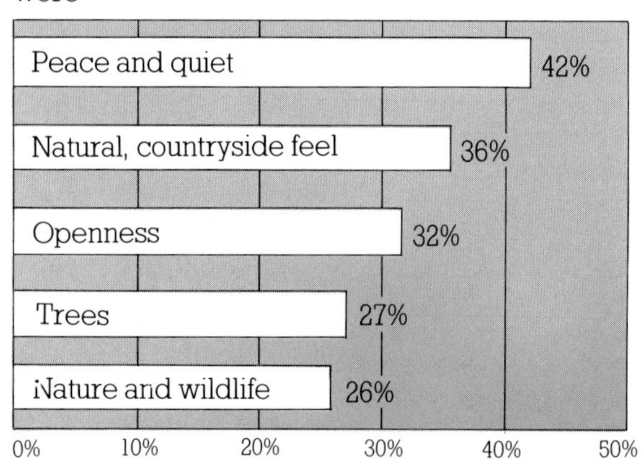

These responses accounted for 50% of the total of positive responses about the sites of which there were 36 different reasons given. Typical comments from the group discussions included –

> "An escape from the zooming cars; it's like being in the country."

> "It helps mentally, you relieve the stress of the day."

> "If you're depressed and fed up it's a lovely place to come; it's more intimate and relaxing because it's not organised."

A natural park also seems to improve the quality of life of the entire local community. Typical of many comments were –

> "If they developed this area (the site) I'm sure the whole community would be downgraded."

> "Before, we were surrounded by concrete; here they want to make a built-up area more rural. It's nice to be among greenery."

> "I don't go over the Park all that often but just knowing it's there somehow makes you happy to live here."

Providers often seem to feel that people are less secure with many trees on a site but 24% of respondents in this study tended to feel that more trees would enhance their site, even Birchwood Brook Park which is dominated by woodland. Apart from the visual effect, many also recognised that more trees would encourage a greater variety of birds.

Previous research suggests that natural landscapes reduce levels of anxiety, repair the emotions and relieve stress. On average 70% of visitors experienced positive feelings when visiting the sites, such as feeling relaxed, happy, peaceful and free. Approximately 15% expressed neutral feelings and 20% expressed negative feelings such as insecurity and loneliness. Only 2% of respondents expressed negative feelings at Birchwood Brook, 30% of visitors to Newbridge Farm expressed neutral feelings such as nothing in particular, fine and alright, and visitors to Gillespie Road typically experienced mixed feelings.

Getting the balance right

The visitors to the three sites did not feel they took second place to nature, rather they felt proud to participate in an environment where the needs of nature and of people were equally well served –

> "I think there's a lot of harmony between the wildlife and the people down there. I think the people living round the place enjoy the wildlife, I certainly do and other people tell me they do."

> "It's well balanced; we want a peaceful place to retreat to and so do the birds and small animals; both are catered for equally."

As mentioned before, many planners and designers, including some of those from our case sites, are anxious about the acceptability of natural open spaces in cities. When asked to describe their ideal open space for recreation and conservation, many felt that they would include a mixture of traditional facilities such as sports pitches, cafes, playgrounds and formal gardens in an essentially natural landscape of mixed habitats. This contrasted markedly with the views expressed by the consumers only 4% of whom wanted to see the parks become more traditional and 10% of whom wanted more facilities to be provided.

It is also commonly held, particularly by ecologists, that big is beautiful and that a small wildlife site will not appeal to people (let alone wildlife) as much as a larger park. Whilst it is certainly true that the small Gillespie Road site would not be big enough to satisfy the needs of someone looking for a long walk, many people felt that they could get to know this site intimately. This was confirmed by teachers who felt that the intimacy was a definite advantage for their children who were trying to learn about the different plants and animals.

A common concern amongst ecologists is that if a site attracts too many people or if people are allowed unrestricted access to all parts of a wildlife site, the disturbance caused could possibly destroy the very wildlife that gives the site its particular character they have come to see. The majority of users (80-90%) were observed to stick to the paths and the ability to walk side by side along surfaced paths which lead to good panoramic views through the sites is much appreciated. Paths must not be too steep, slippery or full of heavy gravel which inhibits elderly people, mums with toddlers and push chairs, people in wheel chairs and bicycle riders. It was seen that the wider the path and the firmer and smoother the surface the more people used it.

Children were the biggest off-the-path users whose activities have been successfully planned for by shrewdly planting thorny plants at Birchwood Brook and the vigilance of wardens at Gillespie Road. Installing barriers, fencing and changing the direction of paths was generally felt to achieve the desired effect of keeping people away from sensitive areas where there is a high risk of disturbance to both wildlife and to residents living beside the sites. Providing small but ample areas of close mown grass as kickabout areas also seems to have been successful at Gillespie Road and Birchwood Brook Park as a way of reducing disturbance elsewhere.

Dogs were of particular concern amongst the providers and consumers of Gillespie Road. An open, ranch-style fence had been constructed across the width of the site between the pond and the rest of the site in an attempt to prevent dogs from charging through the water and disturbing breeding ducks. A gate was provided in the fence to allow visitors through but it appears that many non-dogwalkers had been discouraged from passing through to the pond area which is widely regarded as the most attractive part of the site. The other problem with dogs is the mess they leave. When one considers that one in ten of the population own a dog and one in four of the visitors to the sites were dogwalkers, enforcing a complete ban on dogs would seem draconian, as it would deter a significant number of people from enjoying the benefits the sites have to offer. Various suggestions were made as to how to reduce this nuisance from dog loos to pooper scoopers.

Another aspect of giving people access to nature focuses on the importance of water features. Despite the evidence gleaned from the literature review, the water features on the three sites did not prove to be the powerful attraction we had expected, even though the respondents in the questionnaire survey and the group discussions were very much in favour of them. The mapping studies indicated that less than a quarter of all children observed were seen near water.

Perhaps, as with the sites as a whole, just knowing that a water feature is there is of intrinsic value. On the other hand, it may be the case that people are just not getting the full benefits from these features because access is difficult. There is no path beside the brook in Birchwood Brook Park although children tend to play around the concrete weir. The paths alongside the River Cole at the Birmingham site are very narrow and overgrown along most of their length. The combination of the dog-free zone and only a small frontage to the pond at Gillespie Road may deter more people from venturing down to the water's edge. This is a controversial subject and remains a question of achieving a balanced attitude with the aim of maximising the benefits and reducing the risks of any particular situation. At Newbridge Farm some of the most attractive natural scenery and wildlife was to be found on the south side of the river, but the majority of people never penetrated that area which may suggest that the river is seen as a barrier rather than an attractive natural feature.

Benches, picnic tables and improvisation

Basic facilities such as benches, picnic tables, paths and signs were appreciated provided they blended into the natural character of the sites. The function of these facilities as focal points for people to stop for a chat or to enjoy the view is as important as their intrinsic practical function, but they must be located within the site rather than on the periphery. It is as if people want to become immersed in the countryside atmosphere of the sites, well away from the entrances, before deciding to break their journey. Without such facilities visitors are deprived of opportunities to socialise and enjoy the sites from a different perspective. At Newbridge Farm, where there were no formal facilities provided, some large drain pipes have become a place to meet for adults and for children to play around.

The innovative facilities provided at Birchwood Brook raised more questions in users minds as to what they might be used for than actual use. In keeping with the idea of not wanting to dictate what people should use this park for, the designers had attempted to provide an infrastructure that would lend itself to all kinds of use from a toddlers play group to a drama production, a campfire singsong to an outdoor meeting room. In the event the turf circles and sitting areas were perhaps too subtle and particularly so in the context of a population who may feel less confident about using natural open spaces than most.

It was found that it is the occasional user who needs to know what to do and what to expect from urban wildlife sites, rather than the frequent user or the non-user (who, typically, is a regular user of some other open space elsewhere). Occasional users tend to feel more exposed and insecure, want more traditional facilities and be concerned that more people don't use the site. This is the group of users for whom more could be done.

Playing with nature

The designers of Birchwood Brook Park had been particularly keen to encourage children to play in this park and indeed 34% of all visitors mapped at this site were aged between 5 and 12. Despite this, children were not perceived by adults as main users of this site. Part of the reason for this is probably that the children are just not visible from the main paths and entry points because they seem to choose to play along the edge of the woodland near the housing or else in the undergrowth within the park.

The desire for some or more children's play facilities was far less than might have been expected, being requested by only 15% of respondents in the questionnaire survey. Several respondents in the group discussions revealed that their children find the site extremely attractive and are "never short of something to do there". It also appears that children who are taught about wildlife in schools and through site visits often are responsible for introducing their parents to the sites. As one parent said –

> "You see, we've had David Bellamy here at our school and so our children know more about it than we do. Then the rangers take them around the area which is absolutely wonderful; they also come into our schools."

Comparing the results from the three sites, it would seem that children are more likely to use a natural open space if it provides a high degree of privacy from housing and adults using the main paths; only 23% of users at Gillespie Road were children. The same is true for teenagers who were present in the greatest proportion at Newbridge Farm (21% of all users) as compared to an average of 17% across the three sites. Aside from exuberance when two or more were together, there were some instances of anti-social behaviour observed which, whilst few in number, were more significant in the minds of witnesses. Motorbiking had been something of a problem at Newbridge Farm on one occasion and the rangers at Birchwood Brook reported a problem with glue sniffing and under-age drinking. However, in the group discussions, teenagers described the pleasures of taking a walk in natural surroundings and being able to get away from it all in a countryside atmosphere much as adults had done.

Past research suggests that the aspects of natural open spaces that people disliked, corresponded more closely to those of urban open spaces in general, rather than countryside recreation sites. The responses to the questionnaire survey were –

Litter and dumping	31%
Too many dogs	30%
Vandalism	24%
Uncared-for appearance	17%

These responses accounted for 48% of the total number of negative responses of which there were 30 different answers given.

Litter

Litter always seems to be a problem no matter how much or little of it there appears to be. Users felt that litter indicated that both the providers and other users do not value the site. The providers felt it was unreasonable of the public to expect them to clear everything from sweet wrappers to supermarket trolleys, although they agreed that litter spoiled the visual harmony they were trying to create and maintain. By far the worst affected site was Newbridge Farm where there was no warden and little to suggest that the authorities were actively maintaining the site. Educating the community was seen to be the only answer to the problem, given that the local authority was unable to find the money or the labour to undertake any clear-up operations.

Vandalism

In spite of warnings by managers, wardens and teachers about the vandalism, it was not immediately evident to the research team and in fact took some time to find even on the smallest site. Such damage as there was, a few broken trees and burnt logs, appears to have had an exaggerated effect on the minds of wardens and rangers, in that it may be preventing them from trying to increase use for fear this will lead to more vandalism.

There is a feeling amongst some providers and users that the less conspicuous facilities and signs of management are, the less likely a site is to be vandalised; a point that came through strongly in the discussions about Newbridge Farm. As one user commented –

> "It's better this way, there's nothing to vandalise."

Uncared-for appearance

As mentioned previously, the majority of local people appreciate the natural character of the parks and do not wish to see them evolve into more traditional parks. this must be distinguished from the concerns voiced about the uncared-for appearance. An overgrown appearance, whether bushes, trees, high grasses or narrow paths may be perceived not only as untidy but also as a threat. One woman described Newbridge Farm as having –

> "... an image of a derelict place, a place to get attacked, especially down by the river where there is tall vegetation, people may be put off."

An uncared-for appearance encourages substantial numbers of the public to downgrade a natural open space to a tipping ground. This in turn discourages regular users from actively trying to maintain it, as well as planting doubts in the minds of others about the future of the site. In other words they lose confidence in the site. This was undoubtedly the case at Newbridge Farm to the extent that it had not only affected public attitudes towards the site but was discouraging the local authority from taking on the responsibility to reverse the situation.

Colour

When compared with the vivid displays so typical of traditional public gardens, colour in natural landscapes tends to be more subdued, dominated as it is by greens and browns. Lack of colour is seen as a subject for thought and creative solutions by both providers and users, neither of whom wish to see too many conifers or traditional bedding plants brought in to guarantee colour. Having anticipated criticism from users, the providers hoped that various attempts they were making to enhance colour would be appreciated. These included retaining and adding to the colourful native species and non-native species resident on the sites when first discovered, such as lupins, roses and conifers, and transplanting some of the more colourful native wildflowers. At Gillespie Road the children from the Nature Club were planting a small wildflower garden at the main entrance with an emphasis on colour. Frequent users, who were the keen observers of nature, were appreciative of the variety of colours to be seen in the wildflowers, birds and butterflies on their sites and were less concerned about this issue. None the less, there was a widespread desire for more wildlife to be encouraged to inhabit all three sites.

Promoting the sites to the public

Providers assume that the public must be introduced to natural open spaces via special social and cultural events, guided walks, talks or rangers and wardens on the site. Such a programme of events was available at Birchwood Brook Park and the manager and wardens at Gillespie Road were just beginning to tackle this problem with a few events for children. However, they felt that they had "a long way to go to bring the park to everyone's attention".

A site's value is enhanced for the provider and the user when it has a high profile within the community. Given the general feeling that usage on all three sites was low, everyone wanted more publicity, using local newspapers, and permanent posters within the community to promote the site – the name, the purpose, who has responsibility for it and the hours of opening. Several respondents indicated that they had found it difficult to locate the sites and to convince themselves that they were in the right place when they did find an entrance. The same would be true of many such urban wildlife sites around the country, as they often seem to be tucked away behind housing estates, alongside railway lines or derelict land. Large attractive signs at the entrances and along roads leading to the sites were regarded as a partial answer to the problem. It was felt that such efforts would not only increase awareness amongst the public but also improve a site's image in the eyes of the community.

In group discussions people realised that should the authorities believe the site to be under-used, and therefore undervalued by the local community then they would be more likely to permit development for housing or industry than might otherwise be the case. Infrequent usage does not seem to be symptomatic of indifference towards a site. Knowing the site is there to retreat to, gives people both reassurance and a strong sense of identity with the community –

> "Just to look out the window and know it's there is wonderful, even if you don't use it a lot, it's yours."

Both existing and potential visitors were reluctant to become too involved and dependent on a site, especially if it appears to be under-used –

> "One hears that the Cole Valley is being developed; what does that mean for our area (site)?"

> "This park is on a lease from British Rail, so it's not very secure; in several years there may be something else they want to put here."

> "If this site isn't attractive to more people, what happens to it once the Corporation goes; after all it's spare land?"

Even frequent users did not necessarily visit a site more than twice a week and yet the thought that the site might disappear was greeted with anxiety and anger –

> "They would have a fight on their hands."

Interestingly, the most tailor-made and well managed site may encourage the most criticism, rather than the more informal site, simply because the presence of an authority, like a new town corporation, which is seen to be well resourced, raises expectations and invites disappointment when these are not realised. The new-town respondents expressed more unfulfilled needs than any other group. They wanted to see more lighting, better drainage of the brook, insect control, an old windmill rebuilt, supervision for the children, more benches and picnic tables, a water point, tennis courts, playgrounds and more activities for the community. All this despite the fact that although the site was meant to be little more than a walkway it was none the less rangered and had more organised activities provided than either of the other two sites under consideration.

Confidence

Whether or not a person feels attracted to visit a natural open space and to get the most out of it seems to depend on a number of factors all of which engender a feeling of confidence. First, the person must feel welcomed into the site through an attractive entrance point. Secondly, they may need to feel that they understand that these urban wildlife sites offer a countryside-like experience and what that means in terms of informal recreation and contact with nature. Thirdly, they might wish to feel that the site belongs to them, rather than to the local authority, so that they feel free to use the sites as they wish rather than as they feel they ought. Fourthly, the need to feel that the site is being cared for sympathetically, that it has some permanence and that there is a presence there so as to promote feelings of security and safety. This fourth point, when compared to point three, raises a dilemma for the authorities.

Just how tidy a site needs to be or how visible rangers need to be is difficult to decide. There can be no absolute standard regarding the most popular and essential features that a natural open space should have in order to be deemed a success. Each site has to be assessed in ecological and social terms within its own specific physical setting and community, bearing in mind that the end result should be a site where the visitors feel comfortable and unrestricted. The effect of a natural open space is to communicate that it is different from a traditional park and more like the countryside. The specific landscape features such as trees, water, shrubs and flowers are not as important as the overall natural effect. Peace and quiet, openness, visual diversity are all important, and the feeling of harmony with nature inspired by sharing the site with wildlife, is more important than the numbers of benches, wildflowers and shrubs.

Issues raised

From our results there would appear to be a greater public demand for natural open spaces in urban areas than providers may realise or, indeed, be able to supply in the medium term. A nature park or reserve was the second most preferred type of open space after the traditional park. And, where respondents were asked what their ideal urban open space would be the non-users of the case sites (who generally lived furthest away from them) selected nature park/ reserve as their first choice. This may be another example of the intrinsic value of a site to the community, even if it is not heavily used by all enthusiasts.

There was some discussion concerning suitability of names such as ecological park and nature park. It was felt that such titles should not be used if there was a chance that they would deter people.

No clear consensus emerged as to how much an authority could depend upon community involvement to maintain this type of site. The providers of Newbridge Farm felt that the only hope of really improving the uncared for appearance of this site was to involve the community in periodic clean-ups, there being no alternative resources available. On the other hand the rangers at Birchwood Brook had been disappointed in the low level of participation on similar events.

Our findings result from an investigation of several thousand people, but only from three sites. More research is undoubtedly needed to confirm these findings and explore other important questions. For example, we need to know how the views and feelings which users have towards the natural open spaces compare with those for traditional parks. We need to know how to promote and increase use of these sites but not beyond the point at which the wildlife, the peace and quiet and sense of escape people seek to enjoy, is destroyed. Finally, we need to know whether the results of this kind of investigation encourage planners and designers to stand up to criticism and make them less fearful and apologetic about asking for the necessary resources to create, enhance and manage natural open spaces.

Appendix

Methodology

The research was based on case studies of three sites: Gillespie Road Park, Islington, Newbridge Farm Recreation Ground, Birmingham, and Birchwood Brook Park, Warrington New Town, maps of which are provided at the end of this summary.

The theories which this research sought to test emerged from a literature review of over 500 references undertaken before the research began, and an analysis of what the site providers had hoped to achieve and expected to hear from the public.

Environments mean different things to different people. When the environment being studied is also of a relatively new type, the research methods must allow for the fact that people may not know how to express their attitudes and feelings about the environment. For this reason a combination of qualitative and quantitative techniques were used, brief details of which follow.

A total of 2500 users and potential users were involved. Group discussions with 56 local residents sought in-depth information on the feelings, perceptions and experience of visitors and the questionnaire surveys provided numerical attitude values from 310 respondents. Mapping of 2000 visitors, according to sex, age group, activity and location on the sites, provided numerical data on the actual level and pattern of usage. Tracking 66 individual visitors over a maximum of 30 minutes, recording their movements and the degree to which they took an interest in the natural elements of the sites, revealed an in-depth understanding of the quality of their experience. The field work was carried out in 1987.

A total of 31 planners, landscape designers, landscape managers, nature conservationists, rangers, teachers and youth workers, who had been involved in the design and management of the sites, were interviewed individually at the beginning of the research and were asked to respond to comments and suggestions from the consumers in feedback questionnaire at the end of the research.

Birchwood Brook Park

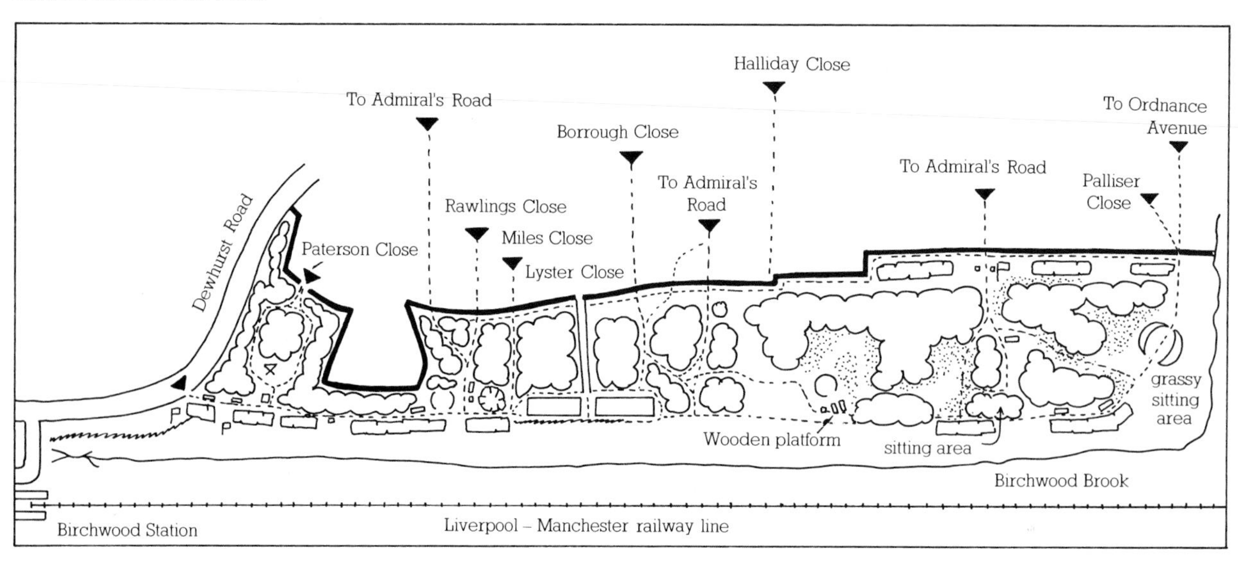

Gillespie Park

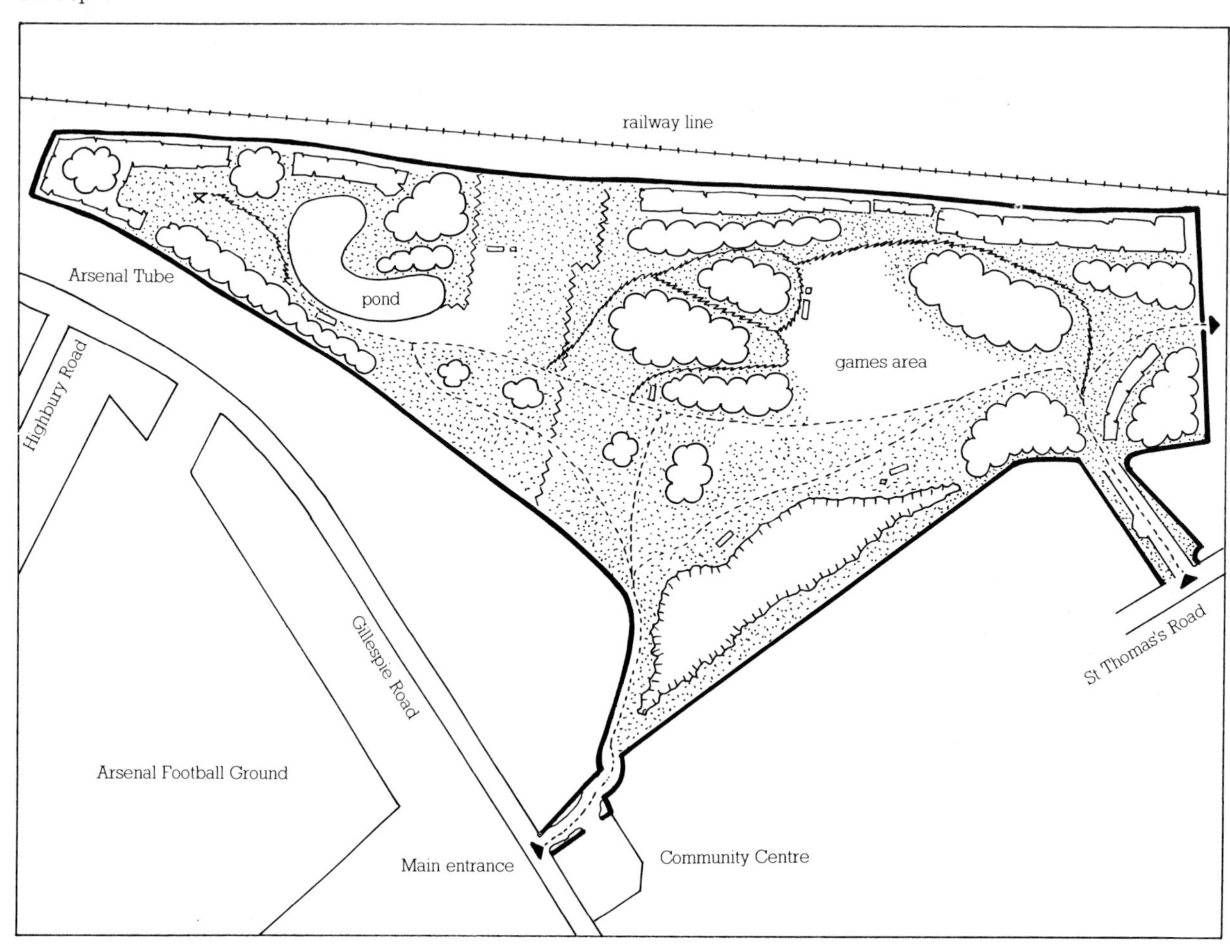

Newbridge Farm Recreation Ground

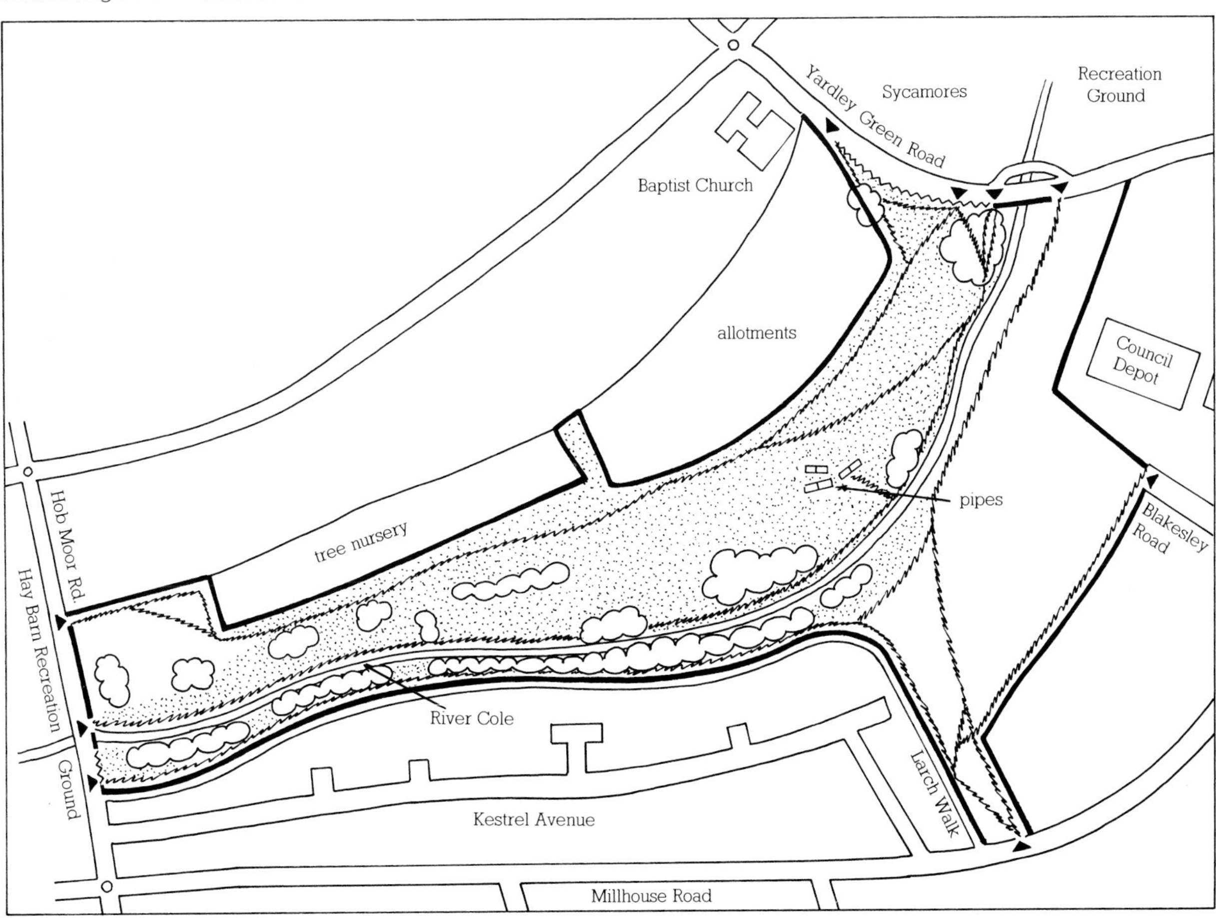

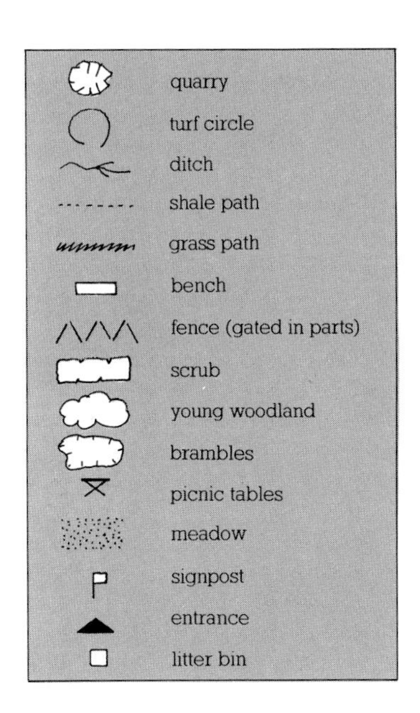